DESTINATION
Middle Ages

Your Guide to Medieval Society

Rachel Stuckey

Crabtree Publishing Company
www.crabtreebooks.com

Crabtree Publishing Company
www.crabtreebooks.com

Author: Rachel Stuckey

Managing Editor: Tim Cooke

Designer: Lynne Lennon

Picture Manager: Sophie Mortimer

Design Manager: Keith Davis

Editorial Director: Lindsey Lowe

Children's Publisher: Anne O'Daly

Crabtree Editorial Director: Kathy Middleton

Crabtree Editor: Petrice Custance

Proofreader: Wendy Scavuzzo

**Production coordinator
and prepress technician:** Tammy McGarr

Print coordinator: Margaret Amy Salter

Written and produced for Crabtree Publishing Company
by Brown Bear Books

Photographs (t=top, b=bottom, l=left, r=right, c=center):
Front Cover: National Archives: Perot Foundation/David Mark
Rubenstein br; **Public Domain:** Biblioteca Marciana l;
Thinkstock: istockphoto tr, cr.

Interior: **123rf:** Alexandra Reinwald 16; **Alamy:** Lebrecht Music
and Arts Photo Library 14r, Lordprice Collection 18, Mary Evans
Picture Library 27l; **Bridgeman Art Library:** 12, 17, 25b;
Dreamstime: 24b, R. Hallam 20r, Dmitry Yakovlev 5b; **Getty
Images:** Corbis Historical/Leemage 24t, DEA/M. Seemuler 19b,
Hulton Archive/Fototeca Storica Nazionale 15tr; **Library of
Congress:** 17l; **Metropolitan Museum of Art:** 20bl; **Public Domain:**
Bede/Imperial Treasury 11t, Bibliothéque Nationale de France 28,
British Library 9br, 25t, Detroit Institute of Arts 13t, Kunsthistorisches
Museum 22, Petar Milosevic 10, Lucien Musset's Bayeux Tapestry
14bl; **Rijksmuseum:** 27tr, City of Amsterdam/A. van der Hoop
Bequest 23t; **Shutterstock:** Zvonimir Atletic 26, ESB Professional
11b, Tupungato 4, Wolfgang Zwanzger 13bl; **Thinkstock:** Dorling
Kindersley 29, istockphoto 8, 9cl, 15b; Topfoto: Granger Collection
23b, Stapleton Collection 19t, ullsteinbild 5t.

All other photos, artwork and maps, **Brown Bear Books**.

Brown Bear Books has made every attempt to contact the
copyright holder. If you have any information please contact
licensing@brownbearbooks.co.uk

Library and Archives Canada Cataloguing in Publication

Stuckey, Rachel, author
        Your guide to Medieval society / Rachel Stuckey.

(Destination: Middle Ages)
Includes index.
Issued in print and electronic formats.
ISBN 978-0-7787-2991-4 (hardcover).--
ISBN 978-0-7787-2997-6 (softcover).--
ISBN 978-1-4271-1864-6 (HTML)

    1. Civilization, Medieval--Juvenile literature. 2. Middle Ages--
Juvenile literature. 3. Europe--History--476-1492--Juvenile literature.
4. Europe--Social life and customs--Juvenile literature. I. Title.

CB351.S775 2017   j940.1   C2016-907391-2
                                                         C2016-907392-0

Library of Congress Cataloging-in-Publication Data

Names: Stuckey, Rachel, author.
Title: Your guide to medieval society / Rachel Stuckey.
Description: New York : Crabtree Publishing Company, 2017. |
    Series: Destination: Middle Ages | Includes index.
Identifiers: LCCN 2017000474 (print) | LCCN 2017001780 (ebook) |
    ISBN 9780778729914 (reinforced library binding : alk. paper) |
    ISBN 9780778729976 (pbk. : alk. paper) |
    ISBN 9781427118646 (Electronic HTML)
Subjects: LCSH: Civilization, Medieval--Juvenile literature. | Kings and
    rulers, Medieval--Juvenile literature. | Middle Ages--Juvenile literature.
    | Cities and towns, Medieval--Juvenile literature.
Classification: LCC D117 .S88 2017 (print) | LCC D117 (ebook) |
    DDC 940.1--dc23
LC record available at https://lccn.loc.gov/2017000474

Crabtree Publishing Company
www.crabtreebooks.com   1-800-387-7650

Printed in Canada/032017/BF20170111

**Published in Canada
Crabtree Publishing**
616 Welland Ave.
St. Catharines, ON
L2M 5V6

**Published in the United States
Crabtree Publishing**
PMB 59051
350 Fifth Avenue, 59th Floor
New York, New York 10118

**Published in the United Kingdom
Crabtree Publishing**
Maritime House
Basin Road North, Hove
BN41 1WR

**Published in Australia
Crabtree Publishing**
3 Charles Street
Coburg North
VIC, 3058

Contents

Before We Start

Medieval society was shaped by the religion, politics, and economics of the time. Society changed greatly over the 1,000-year period of the Middle Ages.

EMERGENCE OF EUROPE

+ **From backwater to world power**

Europe was ruled from Rome (above) until Rome was overthrown by Germanic peoples in 476. The defeat of Rome left Europe weak compared to empires in Asia and Africa. Rulers in different parts of Europe often fought one another. During the Middle Ages, however, strong **kingdoms** emerged in Europe. By the 1500s, European kingdoms were exploring and conquering foreign lands. Europeans had become influential around the world.

A RURAL SOCIETY

☛ **Land means power**

☛ **European cities lag behind**

Most people in medieval Europe lived in rural areas, or villages in the countryside. They worked the land to grow crops and raise animals for food. They also used natural **resources** such as timber for construction. Europe had few cities, but other parts of the world had huge urban, or city, centers. These cities included Constantinople in modern Turkey, Baghdad in Iraq, Cairo in Egypt, and Chang'an in China.

A FAMILY AFFAIR
✦ **Rulers found dynasties**

✦ **Families hold the throne**

In the early Middle Ages, modern countries did not exist in Europe. Kings or queens ruled territories with the help of powerful **nobles**, such as dukes and barons (left). As kings conquered more lands, they created **empires**. Rulers began to pass their crowns on to their **heirs**. This created dynasties, or series of rulers from the same family. Having stable rulers helped lay the foundation for modern countries as the borders of kingdoms became fixed.

AGE OF FAITH

+ **Religion shapes society**

The Middle Ages are sometimes called the Age of Faith. The Catholic Church in Rome controlled the **spiritual** lives of European Christians. Meanwhile, Islam was spreading through Asia and Africa, and even to Spain in Europe. People fought many wars in the name of religion—but religion also encouraged education. Monks called scribes hand copied religious books that were read in churches. People also made great art and architecture in the service of religion, such as Siena Cathedral in Italy (right).

FIGHTING FOR POWER
✦ **Recruiting armies**

Kings and their nobles became important in society by being skilled warriors. The need for land meant that there were frequent wars as leaders tried to gain new territory. Nobles were expected to fight on behalf of their king. The nobles recruited armies from the **knights** and peasants who lived on their land.

Where in the World?

The medieval world was made up of three separate religious areas. Europe followed the Roman Catholic form of Christianity, the Byzantine Empire of Greece followed Orthodox Christianity, and the Islamic Empire was ruled by Muslims.

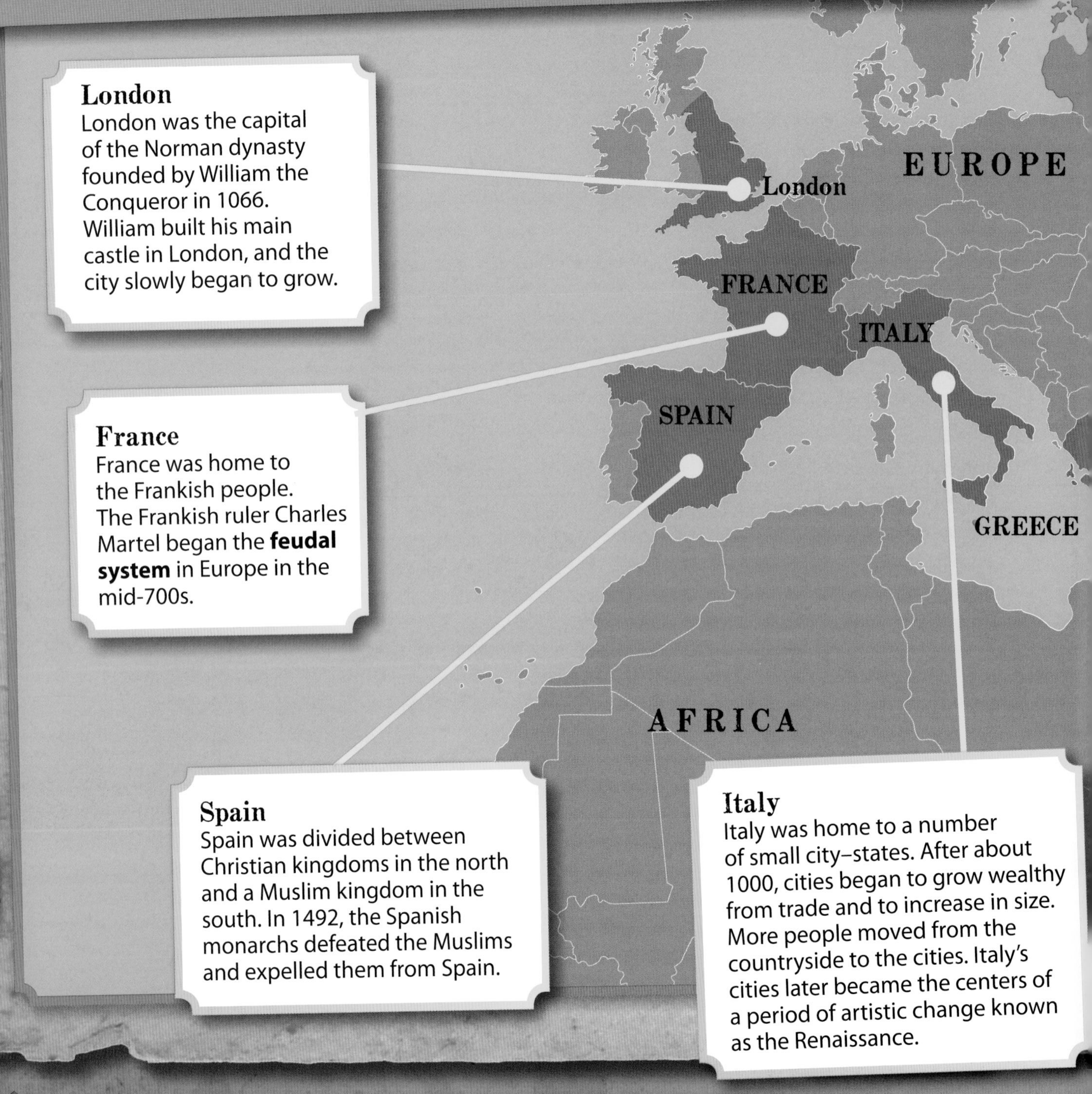

London
London was the capital of the Norman dynasty founded by William the Conqueror in 1066. William built his main castle in London, and the city slowly began to grow.

France
France was home to the Frankish people. The Frankish ruler Charles Martel began the **feudal system** in Europe in the mid-700s.

Spain
Spain was divided between Christian kingdoms in the north and a Muslim kingdom in the south. In 1492, the Spanish monarchs defeated the Muslims and expelled them from Spain.

Italy
Italy was home to a number of small city–states. After about 1000, cities began to grow wealthy from trade and to increase in size. More people moved from the countryside to the cities. Italy's cities later became the centers of a period of artistic change known as the Renaissance.

EUROPE

London

FRANCE

ITALY

SPAIN

GREECE

AFRICA

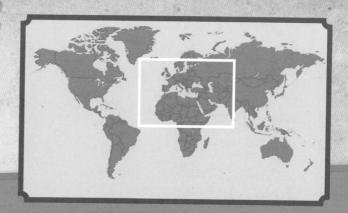

Constantinople

Constantinople was the capital of the Byzantine Empire of what are now Greece and the Balkans. The Byzantines followed the Orthodox Church. The defeat of Constantinople by the Ottoman Turks in 1453 is often seen as marking the end of the Middle Ages.

RUSSIA

Constantinople

B Y Z A N T I N E   E M P I R E

Arabia

Arabia is a large peninsula between Asia and Africa. It is bordered on one side by the Persian Gulf and on the other by the Red Sea. This desert region was home to the Islamic religion.

INDIA

RED SEA

SAUDI ARABIA

PERSIAN GULF

New Names
This map shows the modern names of countries. Most of these states did not exist in the Middle Ages.

Who We'll Meet

Experts today don't know much about the lives of ordinary people during the Middle Ages, as there are not many records of them. However, much is known about the rulers, thinkers, artists, and warriors of the era, and their names are still familiar today.

BUILDING AN EMPIRE
◆ Charlemagne unites Europe

Charlemagne (c. 747–814, right) was king of the Franks from 768 to 814. He was not well educated, but he was smart and listened to advice. He became Europe's most powerful leader after the fall of the Roman Empire in 476. His armies controlled most of Western Europe and Italy. In 800, the Pope crowned him the first Holy Roman Emperor. The empire he created lasted until 1806.

NEWS FROM AFAR

Ibn Sina, also known as Avicenna, (980–1037) was a great Islamic scholar. He was a mathematician, **philosopher**, scientist, and poet from Persia. He was also a physician. Ibn Sina's book, *The Canon of Medicine*, is one of the most important books in medical history. Arabic and European doctors used it to study medicine for centuries.

VISIONS OF VICTORY

+ Joan leads the French

Joan of Arc (1412–1431) was a French peasant girl who believed she heard voices from God. The voices told her to help King Charles VII fight the English in the Hundred Years' War (1337–1453). She led the king's troops into battle in 1429 and won. One year later, she was captured by the English and eventually executed. She was just 19 years old. Today she is a Catholic saint, and one of France's greatest national heroes.

My Medieval Journal

Europe's nobles helped support artists and writers such as Christine de Pisan with money. Imagine you are a noble who pays to support a writer. What sort of works would you ask the writer to produce for you? Give reasons for your answer.

INTERPRETING ARISTOTLE

☞ A great philosopher

St. Thomas Aquinas (1225–1274, above) was one of the greatest Western philosophers of the Middle Ages. He was born in Sicily and sent to a monastery as a young boy. At the University of Naples, he read ancient works that had recently been translated from Greek and Arabic. Aquinas came up with a way of understanding religion based on the philosophy of the ancient Greek Aristotle, which was new to Europe at the time.

A WOMAN'S VOICE

✦ Christine celebrates women...
✦ ...including Joan of Arc

Christine de Pisan (1364–1430, below left) grew up at the French court, where her father was an astrologer and physician. She married a royal secretary, and when he died she wrote poems to earn money. Christine went on to write books about women's life at court. She was also the first to write about Joan of Arc.

A Little Bit of History

Over a period of nearly 1,000 years, many historical changes had an influence on medieval society. Some took place close to home, but others happened far away.

THE BYZANTINE EMPIRE
✦ Ancient Rome lives on

After the fall of the western Roman Empire, the eastern Roman Empire survived. Known as the Byzantine Empire, it was based in Constantinople (now Istanbul in Turkey). The Byzantines spoke Greek instead of Latin, and they developed their own faith, called Orthodox Christianity. In the 6th century, the Byzantine emperor Justinian I and empress Theodora (right, in brown) ruled over the entire Mediterranean.

Did you know?

The Code of Justinian was a collection of Byzantine laws from the 500s. The laws became the basis of legal systems later used in Europe and around the world.

NEWS FROM AFAR

The Prophet Muhammad began preaching the word of God in 610 in Mecca in Arabia. He gathered followers, who wrote the Koran, the holy book of the new religion. They built a **mosque** in Mecca. Muhammad united the tribes of Arabia and his teachings spread. Arab traders introduced the Koran to Asia and Africa, and soon empires and kingdoms adopted Islam as their religion.

THE HOLY ROMAN EMPIRE

+ A Christian empire...

+ ...modeled on ancient Rome

> *" Bishops should despise this world and inspire others by their example to seek after heavenly things. "*

Charlemagne criticizes attempts by churchmen in Germany to challenge his power.

In an attempt to recreate the Roman Empire, the Pope crowned Charlemagne as Holy Roman Emperor in 800. Later, the Holy Roman Empire became a collection of kingdoms in central Europe. The emperor was selected from the rulers of these kingdoms, but he did not have any real control. The kings and princes of the empire's kingdoms had the true power.

A Long War

The Hundred Years' War lasted from 1337 to 1453. The kings of England and France fought for control of territories claimed by the English in France.

HOLY WARS

☛ **Europe's crusades...**

☛ **...fail to capture the Holy Land**

From their base in Mecca (left), the Muslims took over most of the Middle East. In 1095, Christian armies from Europe arrived in the Holy Land to try to drive out the Muslims. The wars they fought are known as the **Crusades**. The Europeans set up states that lasted two centuries, but eventually the Muslims remained in control of the Holy Land.

A Place for Everyone

Medieval society was arranged like a pyramid. The king was at the top with a small number of nobles below him. Most people were at the bottom of the pile.

THE FEUDAL SYSTEM

+ Privileges and duties

European society followed a feudal system. A king (right) owned all the land in his kingdom. He gave his nobles rights to the land as a reward for their service. These great lords awarded parts of their lands to their **vassals**, the lesser nobles and knights who served them. Each piece of land was called a manor. Everyone who lived on that land worked in some way for the lord of the manor and was required to serve in his army. In return, the lord offered them protection.

MEDIEVAL DIVERSITY

✦ **Influences from everywhere**

✦ **Strangers not always welcome**

Although most Europeans were Christians, Europe was also home to many other religious groups. Jewish people lived throughout the continent. They worked in medicine, law, and trade. Parts of Spain had been ruled by African Muslims for centuries. Crusaders returned from the Holy Land with African and Middle Eastern servants. Ports were full of sailors and traders from Africa and Asia. Sometimes European rulers forced foreigners, Jews, and Muslims to leave their kingdoms—or to **convert** to Christianity.

Peasants, are you thinking of leaving your village? There are feasts and fun (right), but most of the time life working for a lord is not very rewarding. But now that it's the 1000s, we have choices! Towns and cities are growing bigger. There are jobs for traders, merchants, and servants. If you take one of these jobs, you won't owe **loyalty** to any noble. You'll be paid money for your goods and services.

My Medieval Journal

Imagine you are a medieval peasant who is thinking about moving to a town for work. Write a letter to your parents to explain the advantages and disadvantages of leaving or staying in your village.

Ranks

Great lords were vassals of the king. Other nobles were vassals to the great lords. Knights were vassals to the nobles. Peasants served the knights and nobles.

DIVINE RIGHT OF KINGS

+ The crown is mine!

In the Middle Ages, people believed that a king received his power to rule from God. This was called divine right. Because kings only answered to God, no one had any authority over a monarch except the Pope (left). The Catholic Church argued that the Pope was God's representative on Earth. Popes often became involved in disputes between kings. They helped to resolve arguments about who had the right to become a king.

Rulers and Dynasties

As kings acquired more territory, they became more powerful. Some monarchs began dynasties that shaped their nations for centuries.

THE FIRST KING OF FRANCE

✦ **Capet increases power**

In 987, French lords elected Hugh Capet (941–996, right) as king of the Franks. To begin with, Capet was not much different from the other lords. Soon, however, he began to seize more power. His **descendents** carried on the process. The Capetian dynasty ruled over the whole of France until 1328. Branches of the Capetian dynasty—the Valois and the Bourbons—ruled France until the 1800s.

NORMAN CONQUEST

+ **William claims the throne...**

+ **...changes English history**

In 1066, King Edward of England died without an heir. The Norman duke, William of Normandy (left, center), claimed to be his heir. The English lords instead chose a noble named Harold as king. William invaded England and defeated Harold at the Battle of Hastings. The Norman Conquest changed the course of English history, culture, and even language.

NEWS FROM AFAR

In 1469, King Ferdinand II of Aragon in Spain married Queen Isabella I of Castile. They united their kingdoms and drove out the Islamic Moors who ruled southern Spain. Ferdinand and Isabella united Spain. They were known as "Los Reyes Catholiques" or the Catholic Monarchs. They forced Muslims and Jews to leave Spain (right), and built a powerful empire that explored the Americas.

Holy Shrine
Two of Eleanor of Aquitaine's sons ruled England: Richard I and John I. The Plantagenet dynasty Eleanor founded ruled England until 1485.

A POWERFUL QUEEN

☛ **Eleanor rules France...**

☛ **...and then England!**

Eleanor of Aquitaine (1122–1204, left) was the most powerful woman of her time. After marrying a French prince, she became queen of France at the age of 16. She became queen of England when her second husband became King Henry II in 1154. Henry locked her up for 16 years for plotting against him. She was freed by her son, King Richard I, and ruled in his place when he went on crusade. After her son John replaced Richard as king, he made her his **ambassador** to France.

WARS OF THE ROSES

+ **Lancasters vs Yorks**

In the 1400s, two branches of the Plantagenet dynasty, the Lancasters and the Yorks, fought over the English throne. The family emblem of the Lancasters was a red rose and the Yorks had a white rose, so the 30-year conflict is called the Wars of the Roses. In 1485, the Lancastrian Henry Tudor took the English throne. He married Elizabeth of York, joining the two families. The marriage started England's famous Tudor dynasty.

Life at Court

Royal courts were at the center of medieval society. Nobles served the king there, while doctors, artists, and scholars all lived and worked at the court.

HOLDING COURT

+ **Serving the king**

Kings had thousands of servants but the most important were the **courtiers**, who were his closest attendants. Courtiers usually came from noble families. Male courtiers served the king, and female courtiers—known as ladies-in-waiting—served the queen. Nobles all hoped for a chance to serve at court. Monarchs were known to grant land, titles, and other gifts to the men and women who served them well in their daily lives.

ROYAL PALACES

✦ **More comfortable homes**

✦ **A great Spanish example**

After about 1300, Europe grew more peaceful. Kings and nobles stopped building fortified castles for protection. Instead, they built palaces such as Hampton Court in England (above). These were luxurious homes that showed off the owner's wealth. These palaces had space for the ruler and his whole court, with rooms for official business and apartments for the royal family. One of the greatest medieval palaces was the Alhambra in Granada, Spain. Built by Islamic rulers, the Alhambra had many buildings with courtyards, fountains, and beautiful mosaics.

ON THE ROAD

✦ **Rulers tour their lands**

✦ **A chance to save money**

On a royal progress, the whole court traveled with the king in a huge procession. The monarch often made a spectacular entry into a town or city, so his subjects could see him (below). Sometimes the king stayed at one of his own castles or palaces. At other times, he stayed in the homes of his great lords. One reason monarchs went on a progress was financial. Paying for the whole court was expensive. A progress gave the king a chance to force one of his nobles to pay the bill instead.

MY MEDIEVAL JOURNAL

Imagine you are a wealthy noble and you hear that the king and court are coming to visit your home. Using what you know about royal progresses from these pages, how would you react to news of the visit? Give reasons for your answer.

COME FOR DINNER!

☛ **When you dine with the king...**

☛ **...no one goes home hungry**

Kings and nobles held large banquets (above) to show off their wealth and power. Banquets took place in the great hall of a palace or manor house. The King sat at a high table with his family or special guests. There were many courses of food that took hours to prepare. There were musicians in the gallery, and everyone danced. Banquets lasted for hours, especially when they were celebrating special occasions such as Christmas, a military victory, or a royal wedding.

Nobles and Knights

Most people never saw their king or queen. For ordinary people, the most powerful person in their lives was usually the local nobleman or knight.

ROYAL MINISTERS

- ☛ Running the country
- ☛ Advisors to the ruler

A medieval king did not rule his kingdom alone. The most senior lords served as his advisors or ministers. The leading advisors were known as chancellors in Christian kingdoms and viziers in Islamic kingdoms. Senior members of the clergy also gave the monarch advice (right). Some advisors sat on a special council called the Privy Council. It could make decisions on behalf of the ruler. Ministers often did most of the daily running of the kingdom.

DIFFERENT RANKS

- ✦ Knights like to fight...
- ✦ ...nobles tell them when

Each kingdom only had a few great lords. There were many less important nobles who controlled large **estates** known as manors. These nobles were vassals of the great lords. They usually owed their status to their skill as knights. Knights were expected to fight whenever their lord demanded, so they practiced their skills in **tournaments**. Young nobles became squires. They served experienced knights, and learned military skills from them.

REVOLTING AGAINST THE KING

+ **Nobles take up arms...**

+ **...limit the king's powers**

Early in the medieval age, kings often had little more power than their nobles. They had often been elected by the other nobles. As kings became more powerful, they often clashed with their nobles. This led to bloody wars (above). Powerful nobles raised armies from their own vassals and went to war against the king. In this way, nobles forced the king to limit his power. This led to important changes in medieval society.

Magna Carta
More than 500 years after it was created, the Magna Carta was the inspiration for the Constitution of the United States.

A LACK OF CHOICE

☛ **Noblewomen have luxuries...**

☛ **...but little power**

Noblewomen lived in nice homes, but their husbands controlled their wealth. They were educated at home and some learned to read and write. Noblewomen helped to manage the manor when their husbands were away, but their main purpose was to have babies and provide their husband with an heir. Noblewomen who did not marry became nuns.

Life on the Manor

For people in the countryside, life revolved around the local manor house. It was the home of the lord, who distributed land among his peasants.

Landscape

Europe's medieval landscape was different from today. There was more woodland and fewer hedges. Crops grew in huge open fields.

THE MANORIAL SYSTEM

☛ Lords and tenants

Under the feudal system, a kingdom was divided into manors. Each manor had farmland, woodland for hunting and timber, and pasture for animals. The lord lived in a castle or manor house (right), and his tenants lived in small villages. The lord collected rent, taxes, and labor from his tenants. Tenants had rights to live on and work the land. They passed these rights on to their children.

THE OPEN-FIELD SYSTEM

+ Farming in strips

Each manor had two or three huge crop fields that were divided into strips. Peasants worked together to plant and harvest the crops (left). Most of the crop went to the lord of the manor, but peasants also had their own strips of the field to grow food for their families. The crops growing in a field changed every year. This gave the soil a chance to recover its **nutrients**. One field was left empty, or fallow, for the same reason.

SERVANTS WANTED!

+ **Working in the manor house**

+ **Wide range of jobs available**

Most peasants worked on the land for the lord of the manor, but some became servants. Lords and ladies needed a lot of help in their homes. Some servants helped their employers to bathe and dress. Other servants worked in the kitchen (right), tended the fires, and cleaned the home. Higher-ranking servants looked after the lord's business, carried messages, or cared for the lord's children.

BREAKING NEWS

Have you had a visit yet? The king's clerks are visiting every village in England (left). They want to find out how much business and farming is done in each place. The survey began in 1086, when William the Conqueror wanted to find out about his kingdom. He is likely to use the information to raise taxes. You might have heard the survey called the "Domesday Book." That's because the clerks' judgment is final—just like "Doomsday," or Judgment Day in the Bible.

GROWTH OF TOWNS

✦ **Centers of trade...**

✦ **...attract more people**

As people learned more efficient ways of farming in the Middle Ages, they were able to grow more food. Peasants began to sell their extra food at markets. Villages with markets became towns, which grew larger after 1000 and became centers of trade. Many people left the manors to move to the towns. This weakened the feudal system and eventually helped bring it to an end.

Peasant Life

Most peasants were farmers, but others were shepherds or fishermen. Peasants depended on their lord for their livelihoods—but also on each other.

SHARING LIFE TOGETHER

+ The medieval village

+ At work and play

EQUAL PARTNERS?

☞ Peasant women enjoy more choice...

☞ ...as long as they are married

Most peasants spent their entire lives in the same village. People worked together to bring in the harvest, mill grain into flour, make ale, or weave cloth. They also socialized together (above). There was lots of noise from the cows, pigs, and chickens that people kept in or near their houses to protect the animals from wolves. There were constant smells from cooking on open fires, garbage thrown outside the village, and the open pits people used as bathrooms.

Peasant women had to marry men chosen by their fathers. Both married noblewomen and married peasant women were considered the property of their husbands. Like peasant men, women worked for the lord of the manor. The women did more of the domestic work, such as caring for babies, making clothes, and cooking food. But they also worked together with their husbands on the land or in a trade. In many ways, peasant women had more freedom than noblewomen did.

FOOD AND DRINK

- ☛ **There's not much variety!**
- ☛ **Drink ale, not water**

Peasants ate simple foods such as brown bread, vegetables such as onions and carrots, and fruits such as apples and berries. They made a porridge called pottage from grains such as barley and oats. They also ate cheese, eggs, fish, and a little meat. Instead of water, everyone drank a weak alcoholic beverage called ale. They drank stronger alcohol at the inn (above). There were no potatoes, corn, or tomatoes. These foods came from the Americas and were not introduced to Europe until after 1500.

MY MEDIEVAL JOURNAL

Imagine you are a woman in the Middle Ages. Using information in this book, do you think you would prefer to be a noblewoman with wealth but less freedom, or a peasant woman with more freedom but little money? Give reasons for your preference.

IT'S A HARD LIFE!

- ✦ **Backbreaking work...**
- ✦ **...and no chance of change**

Life for medieval peasants was hard. From sunrise to sunset, they worked in the fields or at other tasks on their lord's manor. Most died relatively young. They had to pay taxes to their lords (below left) in money or in goods such as crops. Most peasants could not read or write, and they had little chance to change their position in society. In the early Middle Ages, peasants also had to fight for their lords in wars. In the later Middle Ages, more peasants lived outside the feudal system. They worked for money, but they still had to contribute to the lord's wars or the king's wars by paying taxes.

Fighting Power

Did you know?
The Middle Ages saw a growth of nationalism. This was a belief that people who shared the same background and language should not be ruled by foreigners.

Sometimes people revolted against their rulers. Some of these rebels were peasants who thought society was unfair. Many were nobles who also disagreed with the way in which society was organized.

DEATH TO NOBLES!
✦ **Revolt in France**
✦ **Rebels on the march**

In 1358, peasants rebelled against their lords in northern France. Led by a peasant named Guillaume Cale, the rebels destroyed castles and attacked and killed nobles (right). After a few weeks, they were defeated by the king's armies. Nobles called all peasants "Jacques," and Cale became known as "Jacques Bonhomme" or "Jack Goodfellow." His revolt became known as the Jacqueries.

THE NOT-SO UNITED KINGDOM

+ **Scots fight the English**

In the Middle Ages, Wales, Scotland, and Ireland were separate vassal kingdoms of England. But in the late 1200s, King Edward I of England decided to take direct control of Scotland. Scottish nobles named William Wallace and Robert the Bruce (left) fought to restore Scottish independence. Centuries later, in 1603, King James VI of Scotland inherited the English throne and joined the kingdoms together in an early version of Great Britain.

THE PEASANTS' REVOLT

☞ Wat Tyler leads the way

In 1381, Wat Tyler led a group of his fellow English peasants to London. They demanded social reforms and the removal of some taxes. The peasants took control of the Tower of London (left), and beheaded two government officials. King Richard II promised to make life easier for the peasants. He agreed to meet Tyler, but instead had him seized and killed. The king's army defeated the rest of the rebels. The king ignored his promises and made no changes.

BREAKING NEWS

It seems that Simon de Monfort has started a new trend. This former advisor to King Henry III of England led his fellow barons in a rebellion against the king in 1263. De Montfort called meetings of barons, knights, and town mayors to discuss how best to run the country. Now the rebellion is over, the king is still calling these meetings. Observers believe they may lead to a new government body known as the House of Commons.

A WELSH NATIONAL HERO

✦ Owain Glyndwr seizes Wales

Owain Glyndwr (above) was a noble who served King Henry IV. When Henry treated the Welsh badly, Glyndwr launched a rebellion with help from the king of France. He took control of Wales in 1404, but was defeated by Henry in 1409. Owain Glyndwr was the last Welsh prince of Wales. Today, he is seen as a national hero in Wales.

Leaders of the Church

One of the most important influences on medieval society was religion. The leaders of the Catholic Church helped shape life for millions of Europeans.

A HOLY WOMAN

+ Hildegard of Bingen sees visions

+ Writes books and music

Hildegard of Bingen (1098–1179) was a German noblewoman. As a young girl, she had religious **visions**, and she was sent to a monastery. She became a nun (right) at age 18. In the monastery, she prayed and studied the Bible. The local bishops believed Hildegard's visions were genuine. They allowed her to preach to the public, which no other women were allowed to do. Hildegard also published several books of **theology** and composed music and poetry. Her intelligence and her writings convinced her followers that Hildegard was a **prophet**.

AN ITALIAN SAINT

✦ Spreads the message

✦ Francis lives in poverty

Saint Francis of Assisi (1182–1226) grew up in Assisi in Italy. He learned Latin and French as a young boy, and later served as a soldier. After having a religious vision, Francis decided to live as Jesus had done. He began living in poverty and preaching to the people. This was unusual, because previously most monks and nuns had lived in isolation. Francis created the Franciscan order for men and the Poor Clares order for women, to encourage monks and nuns to spread Christian teaching.

RELIGIOUS ECSTASY

✦ **Catherine converses with God**

✦ **Tries to heal the Church**

Saint Catherine of Siena (1347–1380) lived during a difficult time for the Catholic Church. Two different men claimed to be pope, and the church was divided. She tried to bring peace between the rulers of Italy and the man she believed was the true pope. She wrote to many church leaders and kings and queens. Catherine **dictated** her writings while she was in trances caused by a religious experience. Her most famous work, *A Treatise of Divine Providence* (1370), takes the form of a conversation with God about how to lead a religious life.

" *Who will rid me of this troublesome [difficult] priest?* "

Said to have been said by King Henry II about Thomas Becket. The king's knights wrongly took it as a request to murder Becket.

A CHRISTIAN MARTYR

☛ **Archbishop killed in church...**

☛ **...by servants of the king**

King Henry II of England made Thomas Becket (1118–1170) the Archbishop of Canterbury in 1162. Thomas argued that the Church should be independent of royal control. This began a feud with the king. In 1170, Becket was murdered in his church (left) by knights who had been inspired to take action by Henry's hatred of Becket. The feud between Henry and his archbishop was the first major struggle between the Church and State in Europe.

Pilgrims

After his murder, Thomas Becket became a saint. Pilgrims from across Europe flocked to his shrine in Canterbury. It was said that the dead saint could heal the sick.

A Wider World

By the late Middle Ages, Europeans had increasing links with the rest of the world. This helped to begin an age of European exploration and expansion.

THE KINGDOM OF MALI

✦ **An Islamic ruler...**

✦ **...with legendary wealth**

In the early 1300s, the Kingdom of Mali included most of western Africa. It was one of the largest and wealthiest empires in the world. In 1324, the Emperor of Mali, Mansa Musa I (above), made a **pilgrimage** to Mecca. He took 60,000 men, 12,000 slaves, and 80 camels each carrying 300 pounds (136 kg) of gold. When he returned home to Timbuktu, Musa built a Great Mosque, which still stands today. He also made Mali a center of learning.

BREAKING NEWS

Have you heard the news from Asia? The Venetian merchant Marco Polo has just returned from China. He lived there for many years. He even served as ambassador for the emperor Kublai Khan. Now Marco Polo has written a book. *The Travels of Marco Polo* is a bestseller. Already it has inspired European seafarers to prepare to head west into the Atlantic. They want to try to find a new sea route to China. Who knows what riches they'll discover?

THE GREAT ADMIRAL

- ☛ **Zheng He sails for China**
- ☛ **Reaches Africa before Europeans**

When Zheng He (1371–1433) was a child, the Chinese conquered his homeland in Mongolia. The Chinese took the boy captive, and he grew up to serve the Ming emperor as a naval commander. He led seven expeditions around the Indian Ocean, visiting Southeast Asia, India, and the east coast of Africa. Zheng He's expedition led to Chinese trade and settlement in other parts of Asia.

My MEDIEVAL JOURNAL

Imagine you are living in the Middle Ages when you hear stories about China in distant Asia. What sort of stories would make you think about leaving your home and trying to travel to China? Make a list of the reasons people might make the journey.

THE GREATEST TRAVELER

- ◆ **Ibn Battuta on the move**

The Moroccan traveler Ibn Battuta (1304–1377, left) was the greatest traveler of the Middle Ages. Over a period of 20 years, he visited almost every Muslim country in the world—even China and Southeast Asia. He covered 75,000 miles (120,000 km). His book, *Travels*, is a valuable source of information about Muslim society in the Middle Ages.

REACHING THE AMERICAS

- ＋ **Columbus heads for China**

In 1492, the Italian explorer Christopher Columbus (1450–1506) sailed across the Atlantic Ocean. He was trying to find a sea route to China on behalf of Queen Isabella and King Ferdinand of Spain. Instead, Columbus landed in the Americas. He claimed the new land for Spain. This began an age during which European nations conquered large parts of the world and began their own settlements, or **colonies**.

Glossary

ambassador A government's official representative in a foreign country

colonies Countries or areas controlled by another country

convert To give up one religion for another

courtiers People who serve a king or queen at court

Crusades A series of religious wars fought between Christians and Muslims for control of the Holy Land

descendents People who are descended from the same ancestor

dictated Spoke something aloud so that it could be written down

empires Large areas that are controlled by a single ruler

estates Areas of land

feudal system A social organization in which all land is held in return for service to a king or a lord

heirs People who inherit someone's property and titles after that person dies

kingdoms Areas ruled by a king or queen

knights Soldiers who fight on horseback

loyalty Showing constant support for someone or for a cause

martyr Someone who dies for their religion or another cause

mosque Muslim place of worship

nobles People who hold a high rank in a feudal society and pass it on to their family

nutrients Substances that plants and animals need to live and grow

outlaw A person who has broken the law but has not yet been caught

pilgrimage A journey made to a sacred place for religious reasons

prophet A messenger of God

philosopher Someone who studies the nature of life and existence

resources Useful materials

spiritual Related to beliefs and feelings

theology The study of religion

tournaments Sporting meets in which knights competed at different events

vassals People who hold land in return for service to a lord

visions Dreamlike experiences

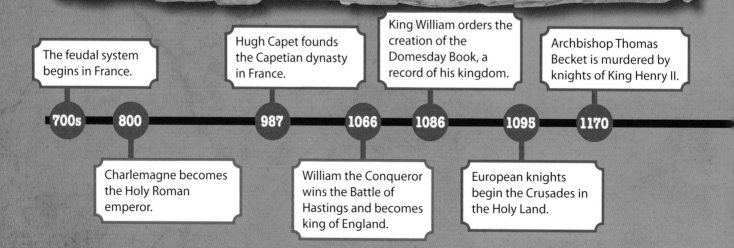

The feudal system begins in France.

Hugh Capet founds the Capetian dynasty in France.

King William orders the creation of the Domesday Book, a record of his kingdom.

Archbishop Thomas Becket is murdered by knights of King Henry II.

700s 800 987 1066 1086 1095 1170

Charlemagne becomes the Holy Roman emperor.

William the Conqueror wins the Battle of Hastings and becomes king of England.

European knights begin the Crusades in the Holy Land.

On the Web

www.ducksters.com/history/middle_ages/daily_life_in_the_middle_ages.php
A page about what life was like for different people in the Middle Ages.

www.historyforkids.net/medieval-daily-life.html
Information about daily medieval life in the countryside and in towns and cities.

www.bbc.co.uk/bitesize/ks3/history/middle_ages/everyday_life_middle_ages/revision/1/
Pages specially designed for students from the BBC History website.

http://medievaleurope.mrdonn.org/feasts.html
A page about food in the Middle Ages and what it was like to go to a medieval banquet.

Books

Allen, Kathy. *The Horrible, Miserable Middle Ages* (Disgusting History). Capstone Press, 2010.

Deary, Terry. *The Measley Middle Ages* (Horrible Histories). Scholastic, 2007.

Hull, Robert. *Peasant* (Medieval Lives). Smart Apple Media, 2008.

Langley, Andrew. *Medieval Life* (DK Eyewitness Books). DK Children, 2011.

Lassieur, Allison. *The Middle Ages: An Interactive History Adventure* (You Choose). Capstone Press, 2016.

Machajewski, Sarah. *A Kid's Life During the Middle Ages* (How Kids Lived). PowerKids Press, 2015.

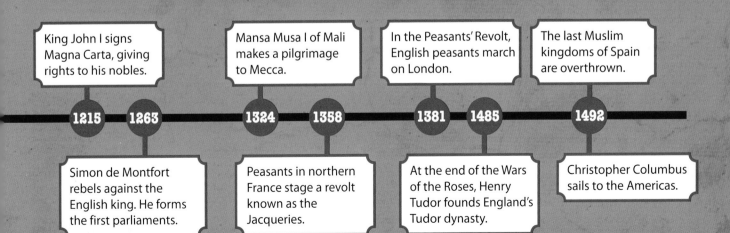

King John I signs Magna Carta, giving rights to his nobles.

Mansa Musa I of Mali makes a pilgrimage to Mecca.

In the Peasants' Revolt, English peasants march on London.

The last Muslim kingdoms of Spain are overthrown.

1215 1263   1324   1358   1381 1485   1492

Simon de Montfort rebels against the English king. He forms the first parliaments.

Peasants in northern France stage a revolt known as the Jacqueries.

At the end of the Wars of the Roses, Henry Tudor founds England's Tudor dynasty.

Christopher Columbus sails to the Americas.

Index